Gash of Newark's Duple Britannia C41F-bodied Leyland Tiger Cub PSUC1/2, 331 BVO, fleet no LO2, new in 1959, pictured out on the road, was probably the flagship of the company's coach fleet at the time of the later of the two visits featured in this book. *(aax514)*

Editor: Mike Forbes
Designer: Debbie Walker
Managing Director: Adrian Cox
Commercial Director: Ann Saundry
Marketing Manager: Martin Steele

First Published: March 2015

ISBN: 9781910415290   Cover Price £8.99

Published by
Key Publishing Ltd
PO Box 100, Stamford,
Lincolnshire PE9 1XP

© Key Publishing 2015

Visit the Key Publishing website at:
www.keypublishing.com

Printed in England by:
Precision Colour Printing Ltd, Telford.

Vintage Bus & Coach

Welcome to the second Vintage Bus & Coach, continuing our series of collectable books, illustrating the heritage of passenger transport in the UK. Our unrivalled access to the 'Stilltime' collection of pictures owned by Chris Hodge Commercials means we can offer and enjoy a large number of interesting pictures of buses and coaches, taken over many years, showing them at work against the street scenes of the day.

Within this book, I have again tried to cover as wide a range of subjects as possible, with sets of pictures from different eras, showing the vehicles of Tilling, BET, municipal and independent operators, featuring both buses and coaches, with well-known types alongside much rarer birds, including as much information as I can about the vehicles and operators, given all the usual limitations. In each category, there are many more sets of pictures for use in the future as well.

The pictures in this book feature some of the vehicles of Southdown, most appropriately in this year of the company's Centenary. Southdown is a name we all know and love and its individualistic vehicle specifications, which were allowed under the less strict central control of BET, always make for interesting pictures. A few Brighton Hove & District buses have got in on the act as well.

At the other end of the scale, but no less interesting to bus enthusiasts, are the vehicles of Gash of Newark. We have pictures of this well-loved and remembered independent East Midlands operator from two separate periods during the 1950s.

Moving only slightly eastwards, we also feature the vehicles of a typical – or perhaps not so typical – Tilling company, Lincolnshire Road Car, are seen during the same period, along with some of those taken over with the operations of Enterprise & Silver Dawn, based in Scunthorpe.

Grey-Green, the coaching operation of George Ewer, will need little introduction, with its regular services from London to the coast. This company had an interesting fleet, running under several fleet names, which are featured here.

We have included two rather different operators which ran trolleybuses. The municipal operations of Derby Corporation included both motor and trolleybuses alongside each other, while Hastings enjoyed mainly trolleybuses, but run by the BET company covering the local area, although as a separate entity when these pictures were taken – in mid-winter at a south coast resort...

Our features Scottish Bus Group company this time is Western SMT, with some interesting pictures taken at the turn of the 1960s, showing then new and older vehicles at work. As with Lincolnshire, we have included a few workshop scenes, as well as buses at work.

We have gone way back in time, with some pictures of the first buses run by the National Steam Car Company, when this operator moved into Bedford in 1919. These contrast with pictures of the Leyland National at the 1970 Commercial Vehicle Show at Earls Court, a wonderful building, which is about to be lost to posterity, in favour of blocks of flats. Such is progress.

The pictures in this book come from the 'Stilltime' collection of pictures from Chris Hodge Commercials. The reference numbers of the pictures are included and copies can be purchased via the website www.stilltime.net

The 'Stilltime' archive contains pictures of all sorts of commercial vehicles, in this case buses and coaches, which were originally taken for magazines like Commercial Motor. There are many more pictures available in all the different categories we have looked at here, plus others, so there is lots to look forward to in further books in the series. One thing to bear in mind with these pictures is that they were not taken by or for enthusiasts, so we get rear views, people in the way and rather more 'candid' shots than might be expected in a book like this, but I feel this adds to rather than detracts from its interest. I hope you agree.

As a life-long transport enthusiast, and spending most of my working life in the transport industry, I have tried to include as much information as possible on the vehicles, operators and the scenes which are portrayed in this book, but in some cases my local knowledge is, all too obviously, not sufficient. If any reader has anything to add or correction to make to any of the picture captions, please contact me via the publishers and we can use your contribution in Buses magazine or a future book, as appropriate.

Editor - Mike Forbes

A Lodekka of Lincolnshire Roadcar Company on a short working of its service 6, just going to Horncastle. The lady in the summer dress and hat is about to board Bristol LD6G/ECW LD60RD, fleet no 2308, KFW 319, dating from 1954, which has the deep grille surround of the first deliveries of the type. In the background is what looks like a Blue Circle Cement Leyland Comet (like the Dinky Toys model), while an interesting pick-up with a canvas tilt, possibly a pre-war Jowett and an old Austin saloon are parked outside the pub across the road. *(aar220)*

Southdown Firsts

This year marks the Centenary of one the most popular bus operators in the UK, Southdown Motor Services. This company has always been a popular with enthusiasts way beyond its operating area in the South of England. Is it because Southdown is associated in our minds with sunny summer holidays on the coast? Is it because of the pleasant apple green and cream livery? Or is it because the company often opted to make the most of the greater freedom allowed by BET to its subsidiaries to indulge in more individualistic specifications for its vehicles? Whatever the answer, it is unlikely that the comparative proximity of Southdown's operating area to its then London offices was the most important factor in Commercial Motor sending a photographer to record the entry into service of the first of the iconic 'Queen Mary' double-deckers, so it is not just enthusiasts who have seen Southdown as a company to watch. So here is a look back at some of Southdown's firsts, along with some other interesting views of the company's vehicles and those of Brighton, Hove & District, long before it was to become part of Southdown.

Southdown was probably influenced by its fellow BET companies like Ribble, when it decided to experiment with double-deck coaches. Its fleet no 700, registered KUF 700, must have been one of the stars at the 1950 commercial vehicle show. The Leyland Titan PD2/12 chassis was fitted with a distinctive full-fronted highbridge body by Northern Counties, with 50 coach seats, roof lights in the cove panels upstairs and rear doors. It was tried on the company's express services, but never deemed a success and remained unique in the fleet, settling down to run on local bus services around Bognor Regis for many years. It did, however, have an influence on later double-deckers in the Southdown fleet. (aar721)

Southdown built a coach station at County Oak on the main A23 London-Brighton road at Crawley in the early 1930s. There was a cafe or restaurant in the building behind a parking area for the Southdown coaches. It was sited 100 yards south of the county border opposite 'Overton's' Beehive workshop.

Unfortunately accidents did occur involving coaches turning right into the park when travelling south, mostly because drivers not seeing the coach signal trafficator arms protruding from the offside.

These pictures show the coach station as building work was being completed. We have a 1931 half-cab Leyland Tiger TS2, fleet no 1044, UF 7344, with Harrington C30R bodywork (which went to the War Department in 1940) and a 1926 Tilling-Stevens B9a 'all-weather' coach, registered UF 1001, which the driver appears to be starting with the handle, also seen exiting the coach station onto the main road, en route for London. *(aah903/904)*

Commercial Motor's photographer was out to capture the excitement of the new 'Queen Mary' vehicles, which first entered the Southdown fleet in 1957. Here, passengers hurry to board fleet no 823, TCD 823, a Leyland PD3/4, with FH69F Northern Counties body, on route 45 to Fareham, under the watchful eye of an inspector and some young enthusiasts. The new bus contrasts with fleet no 253, GCD 352, a 1939 Leyland TD5, with Northern Counties 54 seat double-deck body to the rear on route 45A to Southsea, and the Hants & Dorset Bristols heading for Southampton. *(aat621)*

Above: A great period view of fleet no 823, captured along the route, again with inspectors watching the loading, perhaps because of the change to front entrance. A Guy Arab, fleet no 506, JCD 506, again with Northern Counties H54R body in going in the other direction on route 45A. *(aat619)*

Inset: An internal view of the 'Queen Mary' as passengers board and pass the conductor to take their seats. *(aat618)*

Two of Southdown's first underfloor-engined coaches being launched, probably at Victoria Coach Station, judging from the half-cab coaches from other BET companies in the background. The Duple Ambassador C41C bodies featured a sliding roof between the cant-rail glazing, at a time when, even on vehicles intended for touring, rather than express services, roof vents had usually replaced sliding panels. Southdown introduced a considerable number of these heavyweight Leyland Royal Tiger PSU1/15 chassis to its fleet in the early 1950s, which enjoyed comparatively long lives. *(aba509)*

A Southdown vehicle was chosen to represent what was currently considered the best the public service vehicle industry had to offer at the Festival of Britain in 1951. It was fleet no 701, KUF 701, new that year, an all Leyland H58RD double-decker, seen during the build-up of the show. *(abd028)*

Coming down to earth, but not with a bump. We had to have a picture of Pool Meadow when featuring Southdown buses. Here we have a typical cross-section of the fleet in the early to mid-1950s on a range of the company's services. From the right, 1951 all-Leyland Titan PD2/12, fleet no 710, KUF 710, is on trunk service 31 to Bognor and Portsmouth; next is earlier PD2/1, no 336, JCD 36, from 1948, on service 12 to Newhaven; then 1937 Titan TD5, no 196, EUF 196, still with its pre-war Beadle 52-seat lowbridge body on service 13 to north Moulscombe. On the opposite side are Guy Arab II, no 462, GUF 162, with Northern Counties highbridge Utility body, newly arrived on service 11; and Leyland TD4, no 145, CCD 945 with Saunders 54-seat highbridge body. (aba676)

And now for something completely different...
I couldn't resist including this picture of a solid-
tyred double-decker bus from the early days of
Southdown Motor Services, by the looks of things
an early-1920s Leyland, with a special cargo space
beside the driver. Four milk churns of the earlier
conical-shaped type were being loaded – or,
more likely, as it's on a metalled road, unloaded
– quite a task for the conductor, especially if they
were full... *(aal610)*

A scene at Old Steine in Brighton, with Brighton Corporation fleet no 33, 1939 AEC 661T with Weymann 54 seat body, FUF 33, leading Southdown fleet no 191, a Leyland TD5, with Beadle L52R body, EUF 191, helping to date the picture as, like the BH&D AEC rebuild, seen on the next page, it had left the fleet by the time the Ian Allan ABC was published in 1956. These are followed by another trolleybus and one of Southdown's Utility-bodied Guy Arab IIs, with another pre-war Southdown Titan in the background. (aba670)

Another Old Steine scene, with at least four of the AEC 661T trolleybuses parked on the stand, including (left to right) Corporation fleet nos 3, 35, 10 and 15. Notice that they all carry the 'Brighton, Hove & District' fleet name, not to mention 'Tamplin's Ales' adverts for the local brewery, plus the Standard Vanguard Phase I in Brighton's taxi livery of black with a cream bonnet, seen on the right of the shot. (aba672)

In my mind, it is impossible to think of Southdown without Brighton entering my thoughts as well. This scene outside Brighton railway station shows Brighton, Hove & District fleet no 382, a Bristol K5G, CPN 7, of 1947, with ECW H56R bodywork, next to one of the company's or the Corporation's trolleybuses, with its crew relaxing against the front panel, then GN 6216, one of the early AEC Regents from the Tilling fleet, re-bodied by the company in the early post-war years in ECW style. A Southdown Titan can also be seen to the rear. *(aba668)*

Vintage Bus & Coach

A fine study of BH&D trolleybus, fleet no 341, CPM 62, with Metro-Cammell-Weymann 54 seat body, registered in 1944. It is seen at the stop outside the Tatler Tea Rooms, again on the west side of Old Steine. *(aba674)*

Grey-Green

Grey-Green Coaches are remembered by many who saw them on the roads around London and the Home Counties, especially on routes to resorts on the South Coast and in East Anglia.

Grey-Green can trace its roots back to George Ewer's horse carriage business of the 1880s. Summer services were originally operated to the South Coast, with East Anglian destinations added in the 1920s, then certain services, beginning with London to Ipswich in 1928, began to be operated all year round.

The company continued to expand, only interrupted by World War II, taking over a number of other companies along the way, notably Prince Omnibus Company of Edmonton in the 1930s, Orange Luxury Coaches of Brixton in 1953, United Service Transport in 1965 and Dix in 1976, plus other well-known names in between.

Several of the names and liveries were retained for a considerable time for goodwill purposes and a number of the garages were retained as operating centres as well.

In 1980, Grey-Green was sold to the Cowie Group, and was one of the first private operators to tender for London Regional Transport bus service contracts. When the Cowie Group was re-branded as Arriva, the Grey-Green operations were absorbed by other members of the group and a great name in coaching was lost.

The main base was on the High Road in Stamford Hill, North London, where Commercial Motor visited around 1961, to look at the company's operations, for which this set of pictures was taken, showing some of the vehicles and premises.

One of the latest vehicles in the fleet at the time, a 1961 Bedford SB8/Harrington C41F, 378 BLD, was pulled out of the garage onto the forecourt for the photographer. *(aat614)*

Vintage Bus & Coach

Past the first flush of youth, but still looking perfectly presentable, as Grey-Green vehicles always did, Leyland Royal Tiger PSU1/13, with Harrington Wayfarer C41C body, MLA 195 (Ewer did not use fleet numbers) of 1951 is seen outside the Stamford Hill premises. Points to note are the trafficators, the 'GE' symbol for the Ewer Group on the front panel and the destinations regularly served on the louvres over the side windows. *(aat608)*

Vintage Bus & Coach

Inset: The Stamford Hill 'Motor Coach Station' seen from across the High Road, with the Royal Tiger on the forecourt. Also there are a number of Ford Anglia and other cars, which were offered for hire by the company. One of the ladies from the booking office can be seen on the left, making her way there from the garage at the rear. *(aat612)*

Below: A view from a little further north on the High Road shows the premises from another angle. On the right of the booking office is a 1959 Harrington C37F-bodied Bedford SB, WXC 342, from the Orange Luxury Coaches fleet, which has a board for 'Finsbury Park School Bus' in its windscreen. Other similar Bedford SBs are parked on the other side of the forecourt. *(aat613)*

In more of less the same position as the Royal Tiger, in front of two of the Harrington-bodied SBs, here is 1960 Bedford SB/Duple Super Vega C41F, YXA 374, an SB8, powered by a Leyland 350 diesel engine. The Ewer Group seems to have split its intake of coaches between Leyland 'heavyweights' and Leyland-engined 'lightweight' Bedfords for many years. This particular vehicle is finished in the livery of Fallowfield & Britten, one of the companies taken over by the group. *(aat609)*

Vintage Bus & Coach

Left: This is a 1956 Leyland Tiger Cub PSUC1/2, with Harrington C37C coachwork. SJJ 319 was one of as many as 27 similar Tiger Cubs in the Ewer fleets, but one of just two coaches to continue to carry the Ardley Bros Coaches fleetname on the standard Grey-Green livery. *(aat616)*

Below: Another of the 1956 Harrington-bodied Tiger Cubs, SJJ 301, is seen on the left in this view of the garage, with three or four more in the background, among the Harrington and Duple-bodied Bedford SB8s, mostly in Grey-Green livery, apart from Duple-bodied YXA 373, in Fallowfield & Britten colours on the right. *(aat607)*

Above: An immaculate Leyland horizontal engine is prepared for re-fitting to a vehicle. *(aat 603)*

Left: A man with an industrial vacuum cleaner (and a fag in his mouth!) attacks the interior of a Bedford SB8/Duple in the garage. *(aat610)*

Above: The inspection hatches are rivetted into place in some replacement panels. *(aat597)*

Left: A slightly-scuffed Tiger Cub/Harrington receives some mechanical attention over the complicated system of ramps. Note the large lamp secured to an old wheel. *(aat604)*

The booking office, looking out over the forecourt to the Vauxhall/Bedford dealership across the High Road. *(aat598)*

The control room, where the staff are matching the bookings with the vehicles to be used on the routes seen on the chalk boards around the walls. 'Low tech' by today's standards, but I'd bet that it worked... *(aat595)*

Gash of Newark

Another name which needs little introduction to enthusiasts, wherever they are, is W Gash & Sons of Newark. The Company was formed in 1919, with William Gash using a converted Humber car to carry goods and passengers to market, a familiar story. The main services were to Newark and Nottingham, plus the surrounding villages.

After World War II, the boom years for the company saw it leave Elston and relocate to a new purpose-built bus depot on Bowbridge Road in Newark – which still exists, in use by Jordan Road Surfacing and a car sales company. The following year the business became a limited company with five directors – all members of the Gash family.

By the 1970s, in addition to the established regular daily services between Newark and Nottingham (as well as serving the many villages in between), the company had expanded into providing excursions and tours (including continental tours), as well as taking on works and schools contract services.

William Gash died in 1974, his family continuing with the business, expanding – perhaps too far and too fast – with deregulation in the 1980s. In 1988, with a fleet of 39 vehicles, the company was taken over by Barnsley-based Yorkshire Traction Ltd, at the same time as Lincolnshire Roadcar. For some time thereafter the familiar Gash livery was retained, as was the board of directors, and the Newark bus garage.

Gash buses, with their fleet livery of blue, green and cream, were a familiar sight for many years to many commuters and travellers around the Newark area. The company's Daimler double-deckers also became well-known outside their operating area, being particularly well-kept and long-lived.

Commercial Motor or one of its sister publications of the time visited Gash, and other East Midlands operators, a couple of times during the 1950s, when these pictures were taken of the fleet.

Seen around the turn of the 1960s, on the A46, on the direct service from Nottingham to Newark, was KAL 579, fleet no DD2, a 1948 Daimler CVD6, with Daimler engine and pre-selector gearbox, originally bodied by Strachan, but re-bodied in 1958 by Massey with a highbridge 61 seat body, running thus until the late 1970s. This vehicle has survived and can be seen at the Wythall Transport Museum. *(aax502)*

Vintage Bus & Coach

A view of the Bowbridge Road garage in Newark, probably from the top of a bus. From the left can be seen LRR 403, fleet no DD8, LRR 403, a 1950 Daimler CVD6 with Duple lowbridge body with rear doors, one of two diverted as a result of a cancelled order from fellow Nottinghamshire independent Skills of Nottingham; NAL 782, fleet no DO6, one of two identical 1952 Daimler Freelines, with Burlingham Seagull C41C bodywork, which was withdrawn in 1967, passing to Trent Concrete of Newark for staff transport, which is following a half-cab coach into the depot, to join a Bedford OB, Plaxton, Duple and its fellow Burlingham-bodied coaches. To the right can be seen the boss's Humber Super Snipe car and the company Standard Eight van, 941 ENN. *(aax503)*

Below: A busy scene in Newark bus station, with two Gash double-deckers loading for the Nottingham direct service (modern bus operators would be green with envy at seeing two 'deckers this full, even if it was a special day, Nottingham Goose Fair or whatever...) They are KAL 580 and KNN 622, fleet nos DD3 and DD4, both 1948 Daimler CVD6s, rebodied by Massey between 1958 and 1962. We can just see the rear of a Gash Bedford SB/Duple Vega coach and and a Bristol LS (equally well-loaded, so perhaps they're all going home from Newark's market day) and two L single deckers from the Lincolnshire fleet. Is the schoolboy a bus spotter, waiting to speak to one of the drivers? *(aax504)*

Inset left: Here's a rear view of DD3 and another Gash double-decker, as the crowds board the buses, at the bus station under the watchful eye of an inspector. *(aax507)*

Vintage Bus & Coach

A view inside the Bowbridge Road depot, which ties up with aax503, showing more of the fleet, as a half-cab coach has pulled in to re-fuel. On the left can be seen four double-deckers; the vehicle just seen on the left already has a Massey body; then there is DD1, KAL 578, still with its original Strachans lowbridge body; there is a Duple lowbridge-bodied vehicle in the corner; then DD5, KNN 958, one of two Roberts-bodied vehicles in the Gash fleet, which worked with their original bodies into the 1970s. On the right, the coaches are two Bedford OBs, including B7, GAL 967, actually a wartime OWB, re-bodied in 1952 with the standard Vista body, now restored in the Heritage fleet of Johnsons of Hodthorpe; 401 KVO, a Plaxton-bodied Bedford SB from 1961; a Duple Britannia-bodied Leyland Tiger Cub of 1959 and the other Burlingham Seagull-bodied Daimler Freeline, NAL 783, DO7. These reportedly had vey high driving positions, compared with, say, a Leyland, which drivers either loved or hated. This vehicle is receiving some attention. *(aax508)*

Above: The Bedford OWB, GAL 967, with its 1952 Vista body, is seen out on the road. *(aax509)*

Right: William Gash is seen talking to, presumably, the man from Commercial Motor on the left, of which a copy can be seen on the desk in his office, overlooking the garage. *(aax510)*

Bedford SB1/Plaxton Embassy C41F, fleet no B15, 319 HVO, new in 1961, receives attention in the garage. *(aax512)*

Left: Fleet no DD8, LRR 403, the Duple lowbridge-bodied Daimler CDV6 from 1950, being worked on over the pit. *(aax513)*

Another view of Newark bus station, but from an earlier visit. Here we have DD6, KNN 959, another Daimler CVD6, showing off its Roberts double-deck body, on the Nottingham direct service. On the left, we can see the rear of a Gash coach, DO1 – possibly a Crossley – KAL 737, next to a Lincolnshire Road Car Bristol LWL single-decker, 2039, HBE 756. The Lincolnshire vehicles next to DD6 are interesting, a Lelyand Tiger single-decker, from the late pre-war years and an ex-London Transport Utility Bristol K6A, HGC 246. The road sign shows the A1, north to Retford, leading to the continuation of the A46 to Lincoln, and south to Grantham, leading to the A17 to Sleaford – remember those checked bars on the road signs? *(aba131)*

Again at Newark bus station, here is that Gash coach hiding behind DD3, KAL 580, still with its original Strachans lowbridge bodywork. *(aba132)*

In this shot at Huntingdon Street bus station in Nottingham (more of this in a future album) is one of Gash's Roberts-bodied Daimler CVD6 double-deckers, Gash DD5, KNN 958, ready for the Newark direct run, in front of that single-deck coach again, no doubt on the parallel run through the villages. They are pulled up behind Skills' Duple lowbridge-bodied Daimler, LTO 10, on its way to East Bridgford, via Radcliffe, as Trent AEC single-decker RC 9676 passes on its way to Hucknall. *(aba144)*

A rear view of Gash's DD5 at Huntingdon Street. *(aba146)*

An atmospheric night shot of Gash's DD8, LRR 403, a Duple lowbridge-bodied Daimler CVD6, on its way out of Nottingham on the Newark Direct service. *(aba140)*

Lincolnshire Lovelies

In the last Vintage Bus & Coach album, we looked at some United buses, alongside some from Wilkinsons of Sedgefield. This time, we have selected another Tilling fleet, the Lincolnshire Road Car Company. The company dated back to 1922, when a branch of W P Allen's Clacton & District Services was set up, with services to Grimsby and Louth. In 1926, the name changed to Silver Queen Motor Omnibus Company. By 1928, the fleet had grown to 20 and the LRCC name was registered under Tilling and BAT control.

Various other companies were acquired as LRCC grew and the LMS and LNER railways took shares, with the services of United Automobile Services in Lincolnshire, another Tilling/BAT railway associate company being taken over, notably to the south of the county, as this company's vast operating area was split into more manageable units. When the Tilling and BAT companies split in 1942, LRCC passed to Tilling and so came into the BTC fold in 1948.

Some of these pictures would have been taken during the same visit to the area as to Gash of Newark, but there are also views around Skegness, Grantham, Lincoln and Grimsby, which tie in with pictures of those corporation fleets – perhaps more for next time…

Lincolnshire's territory was largely rural, as was the case for a number of the Tilling companies, which tended to be reflected in the fleet, with plenty of single-deckers, many of which were anything but young. The company also did quite a lot of rebuilding at its Bracebridge Heath works, just outside Lincoln, all of which made for plenty of interest for enthusiasts.

Some interesting vehicles have been caught in these pictures, not only the usual BTC Bristol/ECW combinations one would expect, but also some different makes and models, left over from pre-war days, taken over with other companies or bought-in.

There are also some pictures which show vehicles in the Enterprise of Scunthorpe fleet – Enterprise and Silver Dawn until 1947 – which was sold to the British Transport Commission and its vehicles and services taken over by LRCC in 1950.

Some of the locations of the pictures are pretty obvious and recognisable, even today, while for others I have had to make an 'educated guess', so I hope no enthusiasts with better local knowledge are upset if I have got them wrong. Please let me have your comments or corrections, which we can publish where appropriate in future books or magazines.

Let's begin with a classic Tilling scene, a Lodekka on a trunk route in the country. This is LRCC fleet no 2338, OFU 88, a Bristol LD6G, with ECW LD60RD from 1956. It is on route 6 from Skegness to Lincoln, via Spilsby and Horncastle and has stopped, probably in the former village, to pick up some passengers, while the Post Office Telephones engineer, whose Morris Minor van can be seen in the background, looks on. *(aar218)*

Vintage Bus & Coach

Left: This is Lincolnshire fleet no 2018, FFW 828, a Bristol L6B, with ECW B35R body, dating from 1949. It is on a local service in Skegness, to Queens Road, which is still on the western edge of town, away from the sea. It is pulling up at a bus stop which today might be considered rather too close to the zebra crossing, over which the Morris Cowley behind the bus is passing. *(aar218a)*

Below: Lincolnshire converted a number of Bedford OB/Duple Vista coaches to an open-sided 'toastrack' style, for services along the seafront at Skegness. The fare was '2d All the way - Clock tower to Figure 8' – sounds like a bargain and I'm sure all the happy holidaymakers would know where that meant. This is fleet no 1003, which came to LRCC from Eastern National in 1958 for conversion. Its sister vehicle, 1004, LTA 752, which came from Western National in 1960, is now restored to this specification, with Lodge's of High Easter, Essex. *(aar221 and 222)*

Let's pause for some maintenance: the mechanic is certainly getting into his work, having climbed into the engine compartment of fleet no 2310, LFW 318, a Bristol LD6B of 1954, with the usual ECW body. *(aar224)*

Our man sitting on the gantry is hand-painting an advert on the cant-rail of a Bristol SC4LK single-decker, presumably at the central works at Bracebridge Heath. *(aar229)*

Vintage Bus & Coach

For everybody who has wondered what the drop-centre rear axle on a Lodekka looks like, here is one on the bench at Lincolnshire's workshops, awaiting the attentions of the apprentices, by the look of things. *(aar261)*

I would say this is a service vehicle body being built on the elderly chassis of a Bristol L or similar. LRCC had at least one with front panels resembling the ECW 'Queen Mary' coaches, which this carpenter could be creating, while an SC4LK has some damage to its rear end attended to in the background. *(aar263)*

Vintage Bus & Coach

Top left: This is almost certainly Grantham bus station, with LRCC fleet no 2138, JBE 869, a Bristol KSW6G/ECW H60R, new in 1952, on route 22 up the A1 to Newark, 1956 LD6G, fleet no 2337, OFU 87, on a service to Sleaford, and a Bristol SC4LK in the background. *(aar257)*

Bottom left: Another view of the bus station, with LRCC fleet no 2443, OFW 792, a Bristol SC4LK/ECW B35F of 1957, pausing to take on passengers. Notice how the driver has to twist round to collect the fares. *(aar258)*

A rear view of a Lodekka, LRCC fleet no 2357, SFU 311, an LD5G, with the five cylinder Gardner engine, considered sufficiently powerful for services across the Lincolnshire fens. The conductor, in his summer jacket on the platform, is supervising loading of an already quite full bus for Boston, presumably in the early evening, with lots of young people off for an evening 'in town'. Are the girls wondering if a 'relief' is going to be provided to get them all there? *(aar259)*

Above: A lovely early 1950s view of a country depot. The only clue to the location is the blind for Cleethorpes on the Leyland Tiger TS7 of 1935, fleet no 372, FW 5700, still with its original Brush body (sister FW 5698, renumbered 1411 in 1953, with a new Burlingham body fitted in 1949, is preserved by the Lincolnshire Vintage Vehicle Society). Next to the Tiger is a 1947 Bristol L6B/ECW DP31R, fleet no 685, a pre-war bonneted Leyland Cub, an ex-Enterprise AEC single-decker and the rear of another pre-war looking single-decker. On the right is EFU 855, one of the Beadle single-deckers, built in the early post-war years, using components from 1930s Leyland Cubs. *(aaz834)*

Right: This picture from the early post-war years, I think is in Grimsby, judging from the furnisher's advert on the double-decker. The classic 'Relief Car' in the destination screen offers no help. The two Lincolnshire vehicles are both prewar Leylands, re-bodied during the war to Utility standards. Fleet no 234, DO 8752, looks like a TS2, registered in 1930 while the double-decker is most likely a TD5 from around 1935. *(aaz847)*

We are probably still in Grimsby, with one of the Leyland Tiger TS7s of 1935, fleet no 404, FW 6865, with a new Burlingham body fitted in 1949, exiting the Lincolnshire Road Car bus station on the long route to Lincoln, with a Bedford OWB just visible behind it. *(aaz843)*

This could be Brigg bus station, with the LRCC Tiger which seen in the garage in aaz834 on the left, on its way to Cleethorpes, via Market Rasen, Binbrook and Grimsby, and a Utility lowbridge-bodied Guy Arab II from the Enterprise fleet, CFW 215 (Lindsey, Lincolnshire, 1945), on its way to Immingham. *(aaz849)*

Taken a few mintes earlier, this picture shows an AEC Regal coach, DFU 972 (Lindsay, 1946), of Enterprise, about to leave for Immingham. In the background can be seen another Enterprise AEC single-decker, plus a bus-bodied Bedford OB and a Leyland Cub of LRCC. Is this around the corner from where picture aaz834 was taken?. *(aaz845)*

Left: Next we have a view of the Enterpise bus station off High Street, Scunthorpe, with yet another of those LRCC 1935 Tigers, FW 8827 on the company's stand for the Ashby service, while an AEC Regent, with a Utility body, DFW 936 (Lindsey, 1946) is on the Enterprise service to Yaddlethorpe Crossroads. There is another Enterprise Utility double-decker in the background. *(aaz839)*

Right: A different view of the Enterprise bus station and the company's garage to the rear, showing one of the company's AEC Regal single-deckers, like the one preserved in the Lincolnshire Vintage Vehicle Society collection, with a couple of early post-war AEC double-deckers. *(aaz840)*

To finish, we're back at Newark bus station, with the Gash vehicles discussed earlier in the background. Three Lincolnshire vehicles are here too, a Bristol LS5G with ECW B45F body, fleet no 2205, KFU 361, on a town service, with Bristol LL6B/ECW B39R, fleet no 2033, GFW 851 and Bristol K6A, fleet no 2110, HGC 246, seen previously at this location, also on a fairly local service, to Balderton, to the south of Newark. *(aba122)*

Day out in Derby

Derby Corporation took over the Derby Tramways Company in 1899 and soon electrified the system. From 1932, trolleybuses were introduced, which continued until 1967. Motor buses ran alongside them, with only oil-engined vehicles bought from 1935, Daimler COG5s, followed by CVD6 and CVG6 models after World War II, with only small batches of Fodens and Crossleys in 1952, until the Daimler Fleetline took over from 1965.

In 1974, a year after Blue Bus of Willington was taken over, Derby Corporation was renamed Derby Borough Transport, then in 1977, Derby City Transport, when Derby was granted city status. Following deregulation, with competition from other operators, the Blue Bus Services name and livery was applied to the whole fleet. In 1994 Derby City Transport was sold to British Bus and renamed as City Rider, becoming part of the Cowie Group and again rebranded as Arriva Derby with the corporate livery adopted.

When these pictures were taken in the late 1950s, all Derby Corporation buses were still green and cream, operating a wide network of routes, plus works services and the like. Since then, many of the roads have changed, with by-passes and inner ring roads built, but at the same time, much remains to help indentify the scenes here, which remind us of the days when municipal transport ruled in many towns and cities in the UK.

Derby Corporation fleet no 81, BCH 581, a Daimler CVD6 with Brush H56R body, dating from the turn of 1949-50, pulls onto the roundabout under the trolleybus wires, at the southern end of Corporation Street, having passed the council offices. Derby appears to have been an early convert to 8 ft wide vehicles. What looks like a Trent single-decker is going the other way. *(CHC aba532)*

Trolleybus 181, 1945-6 Sunbeam W/Park Royal UH56R, is seen negotiating the roundabout, with Daimler/Brush motor buses at the stops in Tennant Street and with Corporation Street off to the right. *(aba533)*

Another of the same batch of Daimler CVD6/Brush double-deckers in the Derby Corporation fleet, no 79, BCH 579, passes the railway station, travelling along away along Midland Road (with the destination indicator reading 'LMS Station'!) followed by an early 1950s Morris-Commercial J Type Royal Mail van, OYF 632. They have passed now-preserved former Derby fleet no 172, RC 8472, a Weymann Utility-bodied Sunbeam W4, dating from 1944, and another similar vehicle, with fleet no 222, one of the later 1952-3 Sunbeam F4 trolleybuses with Willowbrook/Brush H60R body pulling out behind, ahead of Derby fleet no 24, ACH 624, an earlier Daimler CVD6 with Brush H30/26R body, from the end of 1947. *(CHC aba535)*

Left: Not the best of pictures, taken through glass into the sun, but it shows a later Daimler in the Derby fleet, no 122, KRC 122, from 1957, a CVG6 with Park Royal H61R bodywork, passing trolleybus 222, DRC 222, the 1952-3 Sunbeam F4, with Willowbrook/Brush H60R, with damage to its roof, seen in aba535, coming out of London Road. On the other side of the CVG6 is Ye Olde Neptune Hotel, which is still there in Osmaston Road, Derby. *(CHC aba536)*

Right: The actual location of this picture is difficult to pinpoint, with the many changes that have been made to Derby's roads over the years, but it shows fleet no 109, CRC 909, a Foden PVD6 with Brush H56R body, one of five new in 1951, on route 40 to Market Place, where the CVG6 in aba536 was headed on route 88. *(CHC aba537)*

The Foden can just be seen in the distance in this shot of trolleybus fleet no 208, ARC 508, another Sunbeam F4, with BTH electrical equipment and Brush H56R body, new at the turn of 1948-49, on route 22, to Prince Charles Drive, via Ashbourne Road, so presumably heading northwards. *(aba538)*

Above: Three Derby vehicles are seen in the Market Place. The driver is just getting into fleet no 122, KRC 122, a 1957 Daimler CVG6/Park Royal H61R (also seen in aba541), about to set off on route 88 to Sinfin Lane. Behind is trolleybus 190, ARC 490, a 1948 Sunbeam F4 with Brush H56R body, just arrived on route 60, with fleet no 106, CRC 906, another of the Foden PVD6/Brush H56R, about to turn into the bus stands. Notice the advert for Offilers' stout from the local brewery on its side and the 'Circular Tour' sign in the inspectors' hut. *(CHC aba546)*

Left: One of the earliest motor buses in the Derby fleet at the time, fleet no 23, ACH 623, a Daimler CVD6/Brush H56R of 1947, one of the last 7 ft 6 in wide buses to join the fleet, has a wash and brush up at the depot. *(CHC aba544)*

Vintage Bus & Coach

Above: Like the Fodens, Derby's Crossleys did not last as long as the Daimlers in the fleet. Here fleet no 113, CRC 913, a Brush H30/26R bodied Crossley DD42/8A of 1952, makes a right tunr on route 77 to Max Road in the north-east of the city. Similar Derby 111, CRC 911, is now preserved at the Tameside Transport Collection. Other Derby vehicles, including several trolleybuses can be seen in the background of this busy city-centre scene. *(CHC aba545)*

Left: A busy scene when the main A6, north from London, to Matlock and Manchester, not to mention the A38 to Burton, A52 to Ashbourne and A50 to Uttoxeter all went straight through the central shopping streets of Derby. We can see, coming towards the camera, trolleybus fleet no 234, DRC 234, a 1953 Sunbeam F4/Willowbrook-Brush H60R on route 22 to the Mackworth Estate, via London Road, presumably heading south, passing motor bus fleet no 122, KRC 122, a 1957 Daimler CVG6/Park Royal H61R, and one of the trolleybuses, with others in the distance. Notice that the trolleybuses, unlike the motor buses, have the rear dome in the darker colour of the livery – although the elevated shots in this sequence show that they all had pretty dirty roofs. *(CHC aba541)*

Apart from the dirty roofs, the Derby fleet was very well-kept. Here fleet no 82, BCH 582, another 1949-50 Daimler CVD6/Brush, is prepared for a repaint. *(CHC aba549)*

Some of the Derby fleet undergoing maintenance over the pits at the depot. Of interest is that motor and trolleybuses, three Daimlers and a Sunbeam W, are being attended to alongside each other, while service vehicle no 4, ARC 267, in the middle is an ex-war department Tilling-Stevens B20 petrol-electric searchlight lorry, converted to a tower wagon in 1948. *(CHC aba553)*

It snows down south too...

Here we have a series of pictures of Hastings Tramways trolleybuses, taken during a snowy winter day in the late-1940s – perhaps in 1947, when the weather was so bad for so long, the photographer had no option to wait for a nice sunny day...

The Hastings and District Electric Tramways company opened lines around the town and along the coast to Bexhill between 1905 and 1907. The local council had the option to buy the system in 1925, but did not and electric trams were replaced by trolleybuses in 1929.

At this time, with 21 miles of route, it was the longest trolleybus system in the world, but was overtaken by others, so its 10 routes, over which up to 58 trolleybuses worked became a moderately-sized undertaking, which closed relatively early, in May 1959, when a fleet of Leyland Atlanteans and other motor buses took over the services.

Maidstone & District Motor Services had bought the tramway company in November 1935, but didn't merge it until 1957. The livery was changed from brown to green after the takeover, but the 'Hastings Tramways' fleetname remained until 1957. The power source also changed in 1936, when the tramway power station at Ore was replaced by municipal power.

There is no obvious reason why Commercial Motor visited Hastings and these pictures were taken, other than perhaps that some of the vehicles were quite new and the magazine maybe wanted to know why Maidstone & District was investing in electric vehicles for this subsidiary, rather than replacing the system with motor buses – we'll maybe never know for sure, but let's just enjoy the pictures, which include some rare shots of the original 1929 single-deckers. Hastings experts might be able to fill in some gaps, but I've included as much information as I can.

One of the early post-war batch of Sunbean W chassis, in this case with H56R bodywork by Park Royal, fleet no 23, registered BDY 798, built in 1946, is seen heading for Bexhill along the St Leonards seafront in the snow, passing a request stop where, it comes as little surprise, nobody is waiting. *(aan395)*

Vintage Bus & Coach

Spot the difference; apart from the outward flare of the lower body panels, this 1940 AEC 661T chassis, with English Electric mechanical equipment and Park Royal 54 seat body, fleet no 19, BDY 794, looks remarkably similar to its later stable-mate. This one is going through to Cooden, at the western extremity of Bexhill and the system. *(aan396)*

Vintage Bus & Coach

A most interesting picture of one of the original Hastings vehicles from 1929. Fleet no 44, DY 5457, a Guy BTX, with a Rees Roturbo motor and Ransomes Sims & Jefferies single-deck B32C bodywork, seen heading for Langham Road, in the north of the town, on route 6. This vehicle was sold in October 1947 and its fleet number taken by another Sunbeam W, BDY 819. *(aan399)*

Left and below: With the Prince Albert Clock Tower, at the junction of Robertson Street and Havelock Road in the background, we see another of the 1940 AEC 661T vehicles, fleet no 12, BDY 787, headed for Bexhill, at a stop outside the a branch of the once well-known national Freeman Hardy Willis chain of shoe shops, part of the British Shoe Corporation, which later used ex-Southdown 'Queen Mary' and other double-deckers for staff transport at its Leicester factory. There are several pre and post-war cars and muffled-up people about, as it's lunch-time. *(aan397/398)*

Right: With what looks like fleet no 12 still at the stop on the right, its sister, fleet no 14, BDY 789, is seen headed in the other direction, to pass the clock tower, on its way to St Helens in the east of the town. *(aan402)*

Vintage Bus & Coach

Seen in much the same position as fleet no 44 on page 67, Sunbeam W, fleet no 21, BDY 796, heading for Ore in the east of the town, meets earlier fleet no 6, BDY 781, one of the 1940 AECs, on route 11 to Hollington in the north-west of the town. They are outside the Roxy Cinema ant Silverhill, at the corner of London Road and Beaufort Road, where Fludes Carpets now is. *(aan400)*

We are back to Robertson Street and the clock tower, where fleet no 54, DY 5457, a Guy BTX with a Rees Roturbo motor and Ransomes B32C body, which would be withdrawn in 1949, is heading for Hollington, with a good load of passengers and what looks like two inspectors standing rather precariously on the central platform. Following is one of the Maidstone & District AEC Regals with Beadle body from the 1947 'HKM' batch which includes the well-known open-top survivors. *(aan401)*

To round things off in Hastings, here is an earlier view full of 1930s atmosphere, looking towards the clock tower again, with a BSA three-wheeler car passing a couple of Maidstone & District single-deckers at the stop outside Freeman Hardy Willis, with two others in the distance. Its a pity we can't see more details of these buses. *(abd273)*

Scottish Style

The history of Western SMT goes back to the formation in 1913 of the Scottish General Transport Co Ltd, as a subsidiary of BET, as a holding company for various bus and tram operators in the west of Scotland. In 1931, SGT was taken over by Scottish Motor Traction, the oldest and parent company of the Scottish Bus Group.

Meanwhile, the LNER and LMS railways had become involved, so that when Western SMT was formed in 1932, based in Kilmarnock, to take over the licences of SGT, the services of various other local companies were also taken over. Further acquisitions followed, both before and after the war and after the SBG was voluntarily nationalised, notably Tilling company Caledonian and Young's Bus Service of Paisley. Western SMT became the second largest bus company in Scotland, until W Alexander was split into three in 1961.

These pictures were taken when Commercial Motor visited Western SMT at its Kimarmock headquarters and other depots nearby, no doubt around the time of the Scottish commercial vehicle show, when the spotlight always fell on local operators.

The company was well-known for its re-building and re-bodying during the early post-war years, keeping older vehicles going. Unfortunately, these pictures do not show any of these vehicles, but those that are included are interesting, with the latest double-deckers seen on longer distance routes, with older vehicles on local duties.

It has been difficult to pinpoint just where some of these pictures were taken, so local enthusiasts with better knowledge will have to excuse any mistakes. Perhaps you might write with any important corrections...

Nearly new Leyland Titan PD3/3, with Alexander L35/32RD body, fleet no CD1532 (C for Cumnock, D for Leyland), MSD 396 (Ayrshire, 1959), pulls out of Western SMT's Cumnock depot, with blinds set for a long trip to Glasgow. To the rear can be seen one of the AEC Regent III 9612E with Northern Counties L27/26R bodies, delivered between 1947 and 1950. *(CHC aar142)*

A frontal view of another Ayr-based Albion from the same 1949 batch, fleet no AN592, CSD 879. It seems to have reached the 'Burns Monument' on the destination screen as it is at Burns Statue Square in Ayr. *(CHC aar144)*

Vintage Bus & Coach

Above: These buses are collecting school children in Kilmarnock on a contract, which apparently accounted for a significant mileage and passenger numbers for Western SMT. The vehicle at the rear is CSD 882, fleet no AN595 (A for Ayr, N for Albion double-deck) a CX37S Venturer with Alexander L27/26R new in 1949, behind a Leyland PD3. This picture, like the PD3 at Cumnock appeared in the Commecial Motor article in November 1959. *(CHC aar150)*

Left: Three of the Guy Arab LUFs with Alexander C30FT bodies delivered to Western SMT in the mid-1950s, still in original condition and front-line use on the Glasgow-London and other long-distance services, presumably heading for the depot for servicing between runs. *(CHC aar143)*

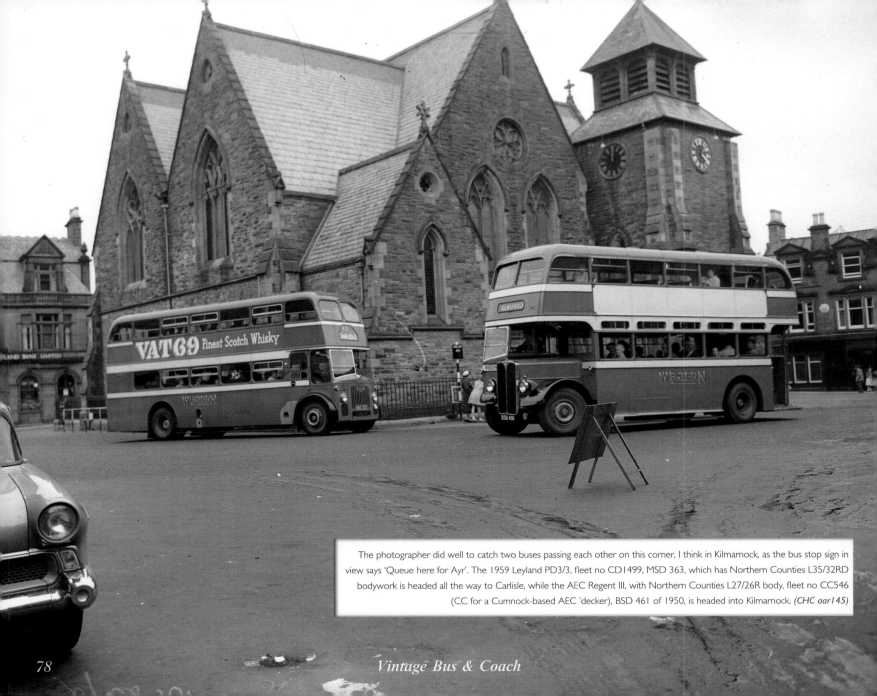

The photographer did well to catch two buses passing each other on this corner, I think in Kilmarnock, as the bus stop sign in view says 'Queue here for Ayr'. The 1959 Leyland PD3/3, fleet no CD1499, MSD 363, which has Northern Counties L35/32RD bodywork is headed all the way to Carlisle, while the AEC Regent III, with Northern Counties L27/26R body, fleet no CC546 (CC for a Cumnock-based AEC 'decker), BSD 461 of 1950, is headed into Kilmarnock. (CHC aar145)

AEC Regent/NCME CC546, BSD 461, is seen again from the rear, at the National Burns Memorial, which is at the Kilmarnock end of the village of Mauchline, between Cumnock and Kilmarnock. *(CHC aar147)*

I think this must be Kilmarnock bus station, where three of the Leyland PD3/NCME lowbridge 'deckers are leaving, including fleet no AD1431, LCS 966, on its way to Darvel, to the east of Kilmarnock, while another of the same batch, 1433, will be headed in the other direction, to Irvine. *(CHC aar153)*

A view inside the workshops at Kilmarnock, with Guy Arab IV, fleet no JY1172 (J for Johnstone, Y for Guy 'decker) GSD 693, from 1955, undergoing heavy mechanical work, with the engine and both axles removed, along with one of the Alexander-bodied single-deck coaches on Guy or Bristol chassis, in bus livery in the background. *(CHC aar151)*

We finish with a bird's eye view of Ayr bus station. At the stands parallel to the road, we can see three of the Leyland PD3/3s, plus a Guy Arab IV —with a similar-looking bus behind it — and an Albion Venturer, all with lowbridge bodies. Another PD3/3 from the LCS-registered batch has stopped in the road, where a lady is boarding while one of the crew climbs up to change the front destination screen. We can identify the other two buses to be seen, fleet no A111 (A for Ayr, I for Albion single-deck, fleet no 11), BSD 281, a CX39N with Alexander C41F body from 1951, and a 1946 Guy Arab II 6LW, with NCME H30/26R body, ASD 851, fleet no unknown. *(CHC aar152)*

National Treasures

It seems safe to say that these pictures of vehicles of the National Steam Car Company's vehicles and Bedford depot were taken soon after the depot was opened in 1919. This was probably in much the same position as the current Stagecoach garage, inherited from United Counties. This is in St John's Street, adjacent to London Road, which still rises over the old track-bed of the Bedford to Hitchin railway line, as can be seen in the background of the first two pictures.

Thomas Clarkson had originally set up the National Steam Car company in 1909 to run buses in London. These were his Clarkson paraffin-fired steam buses. The company expanded outside the capital, first in Essex in 1913, with the operations of the Great Eastern Railway, then after World War I in Bedfordshire, Gloucestershire and the West Country, from 1919 onwards.

The company name was changed in 1919, dating these pictures, to the National Omnibus & Transport Company. Ten years later, the railways bought into the group, with a number of the names we know so well established, later becoming part of the Tilling group, under British Transport Commission from 1948. The operations in Bedfordshire were among those of Eastern National which were soon split off to form United Counties. Things changed again after deregulation, Stagecoach being the current area operator, forming the most recent link in the chain descending from when these photographs were taken all those years ago.

Vehicles from the early 'National' fleet based at Bedford were rolled out for the cameraman. They included this double-decker, which appears to be based on an AEC 'B' or 'Y' Type chassis, many of which were around in 1919, either new or ex-War Department. It was fitted with a body which differs in many details from the LGOC-built bodies on the 'General' 'B' Types. Perhaps the most striking difference is the lack of 'lifeguards' between the front and rear wheels, while there was still no weather protection for the driver. The bus, fleet no 2038, BM 8226 (Bedfordshire, late 1919), carried destination boards for the Bedford-St Neots service. *(CHC aaa164)*

Vintage Bus & Coach

Left: A similar double-decker is seen from the off-side. This one was fleet no 2023, and carried boards for the Bedford-Cranfield service and was pretty filthy from the country roads. There were adverts for Schweppes and a local coal merchant on the outside, plus other local businesses on the inside of the windows. The legal lettering appeared on the side of the body: 'The National Steam Car Co Ltd, Walter James Iden, Joint Managing Director, Office 16 St Helens Place London EC3'. The unladen weight of 4 tons 18 cwt was also on the lower panel with 'FAW' and 'RAW' figures, whatever they were. 'National Steam Car Co Ltd Bedford Depot' lettering can also be seen on the doors behind the bus. *(CHC aaa160)*

Below: There were also single-deckers based at Bedford, apparently built on the same chassis as the double-deckers and looking just as if the top deck and stairs had been left off by the bodybuilders. This was fleet no 2044, BM 8364 (Bedfordshire, early 1920), It had much the same elaborate livery, the same fleet name, legal lettering and 12 mph speed limit marked on the body, with a destination board for George Street. Presumably this was a local 'town' route, ending at the street of that name in the eastern part of Bedford. *(CHC aab023)*

The same single-decker is seen head-on with its proud-looking crew.
(CHC aaa161)

With the single-deck bus in the background, it looks as if the depot manager brought out this charabanc, fleet no 2036, in the same series and on the same type of chassis. They posed it with and without the hood up, in spite of the rather inclement-looking weather, judging from the wet ground. *(CHC aaa162/163)*

It's all hands on deck at the front of the depot, with charabanc 2036, which was registered BM 8227, and another double-decker, fleet no 2041, BM 8250, again with destination boards for Bedford-St Neots. Other boards for this service and Bedford-Kempston are leaning against the wall. The doors are marked 'in' and 'out' and there is a 'enquiries' board on the nearest window-sill. *(CHC aab028)*

National Interest

The Leyland National was launched at the 1970 Commercial Motor Show at Earls Court – soon to be relegated to history, torn down to make way for more blocks of flats – with a great fanfare about how it would do so much for passenger transport in the UK and beyond.

It took another two years before production models entered fleets, and their reception was not universally favourable, to say the least. The National was revolutionary in so many ways; how it was built, how it was powered and its performance, the interior fitments, livery, not to mention the fact that it replaced a number of well-liked models in the wider British Leyland stable.

Of course there were teething problems to overcome. In spite of the rigorous testing from the Artic to the Sahara, all sorts of things went wrong in service. With modifications, as well as all sorts of rebuilds later in life, the National went on to have a long life with many operators, indeed, having a second life with many after deregulation of the industry.

So the model became loved by some operators and enthusiasts alike, but not all of them will remember how the National was first seen by its potential buyers. Here are some pictures of the bus at the 1970 show and others of the 'Suburban Express' being put through its paces by testers on the road and at MIRA, the Motor Industry Research Association's proving ground near Nuneaton, itself celebrating 60 years of vehicle testing this year.

Left: It's 1970 and it's Showtime –with the new Leyland National single-deck bus being launched. It wasn't the world-beater that British Leyland hoped it would be, but it was launched at the turn of the decade to a great fanfare.

As ever with these pictures taken from the balcony at Earls Court, the banners appear to be over the wrong manufacturers' stands. But we can see the Albion stand at the bottom, the AEC stand was off to the bottom left. Then there's the Leyland stand, with the National bus centre-stage and, further to the right Leyland Redline and Austin-Morris stands.
To the upper right, there was the Daimler stand, with the new 'Londoner' – what we'd refer to as the MCW-bodied DMS double-decker for London Transport – and an Alexander-bodied Roadliner rear-engined single-decker.

The crowd around the engine compartment were probably looking to see what Daimler had done to try to make this model more reliable... To the far right, beyond the Austin-Morris vans, can be glimpsed an AEC Merlin single-decker, sporting the London Country – as it would have just become – 408 route number. This is where the bus bodybuilders' stands were, including Plaxton and Roe – who must have been wondering about the future, competing against the National... *(CHC abm035)*

Right: Here's a picture of the National during the show build-up. It was not just the number plate which was changed from 1970 to 1971, the destination indicator which was tidied up and the actual front panel was changed before the show, or at least had some extra trim fitted as seen on the next page. You'll either be most impressed or totally underwhelmed, but it was a brave move, which probably paid off in the end – although not necessarily for British Leyland... *(CHC abl158)*

The Leyland National, as it was seen by visitors to the 1970 Commercial Motor Show at Earls Court. It sat among the various lorry models, carrying the badges of the manufacturers which made up British Leyland, AEC, Albion and Leyland itself, not to mention Austin-Morris and Daimler. *(CHC abh341/342)*